AMAZING ANIMALS

Wild Cats

Stacy Tornio

muddy boots™

we jump in puddles

Lanham · Boulder · New York · London

Published by Muddy Boots
An Imprint of Globe Pequot
The Rowman & LIttlefield Publishing Group
4501 Forbes Boulevard, Suite 200, Lanham, Maryland 20706
www.rowman.com

Unit A, Whitacre Mews, 26-34 Stannary Street, London, SE11 4AB

Distributed by NATIONAL BOOK NETWORK

Copyright © 2017 The National Wildlife Federation

Book design by Katie Jennings Design

Photo credits: p. 1 Pieter-Pieter/iStock; p. 3 (top) MilanExpo/iStock and (bottom) RobinyJ/iStock; p. 4 dptro/iStock; p. 5 Theodore Mattas/NWF; p. 6 Bettyt4240/iStock; p. 8 Kelly Lyon/NWF; p. 9 Torie Hilley/ NWF; p. 10 (insert) Jez Bennett/iStock and GP232/iStock; p. 13 Chrisds/iStock; p. 14 znm/iStock; p. 15 Pile-sasmiles/iStock; p. 16 Raghu Ramaswamy/iStock; p. 17 Abzerit/iStock; p. 19 (top) L Rosebrugh/iStock and (bottom) A.S. Russell/iStock; p. 20 (top) John Hobbs/NWF and (bottom) Sanjdar/iStock; p. 21 (top) Jeffrey Bardzell/NWF and (bottom) Theodore Mattas/NWF; p. 22 FotoW/iStock; p. 23 (top) Kagenmi/iStock and (bottom) John Hobbs/NWF; p. 24 Mark Zborowski; p. 25 iStock and Sandrine Biziaux Scherson/NWF; p. 26 Jirivondrous/iStock; p. 27 (top) StuPorts/iStock and (bottom) Pum_eva/iStock; p. 29 Samards/iStock; p. 30 Luca Lorenzelli/iStock; p. 31 Bridge99/iStock; p. 32 Dimos_istock/iStock; p. 33 (top) Haseeb Badar/NWF and (bottom) Tim Denny/NWF; p. 34 (top) Angad Achappa/NWF and (bottom) Dr. Hermann Brehm/NWF; p. 35 (top) Syafiq_3003/iStock and (bottom) L Rosebrugh/iStock; p. 36 2630ben/iStock; p. 37 Lupos/iStock; p. 38 Mark Malkinson Photography/iStock.

The National Wildlife Federation & Ranger Rick contributors: Children's Publication Staff, Licensing Staff including Deana Duffek, Michael Morris, and Kristen Ferriere, and the National Wildlife Federation in-house naturalist, David Mizejewski.

Thank you for joining the National Wildlife Federation and Muddy Boots in preserving endangered animals and protecting vital wildlife habitats. The National Wildlife Federation is a voice for wildlife protection, dedicated to preserving America's outdoor traditions and inspiring generations of conservationists.

Library of Congress Cataloging-in-Publication Data Available

ISBN 978-1-63076-220-9 (paperback)

ISBN 978-1-63076-221-6 (e-book)

Printed in the United States of America

Cats are some of the most fascinating and mysterious creatures in the entire animal kingdom. From the domesticated cats we have as pets to the mighty lions and tigers in the wild, this entire family is pretty popular. It's not hard to see why either. Whether you think of yourself as a cat person or not, you can't help but admire felines of all sizes for their beauty, grace, and intelligence.

Lions are often called the Kings of the Jungle. They are one of the largest species in the cat family.

CAT ANATOMY

WHAT ARE THE PHYSICAL TRAITS THAT MAKE A CAT A CAT? First of all, all felines are pretty cool because they do have a lot of things in common. Even domesticated cats (cats that have been tamed or trained to be pets) have a lot of similarities to their wild cat cousins. Just take a look at cats—it doesn't matter whether they're big or small—and you'll see that they all have round faces with short muzzles. The muzzle is the part of an animal's face that sticks out and includes the nose, mouth, and jaws. Compared to dogs, cats have shorter muzzles.

On these heads, you'll find very similar and powerful features. For instance, their ears are extremely sensitive and can pick up high-frequency sounds (or high-pitched sounds like a bird call or a mouse squeak) that help them to track their prey. Next, take a look at the eyes, which are large and deep. A cat's large eyes help it take in more light to see—even when it is dark.

When you look at different cat photos, you'll probably notice that some have vertical "slit" pupils (usually smaller cats) while others have round ones (larger species).

This domesticated cat has a rounded face similar to its wild cat cousins.

A cat's pupils can get smaller to control the amount of light that enters its eyes. This bobcat's pupils have shrunk to vertical "slits."

MORE ABOUT CAT ANATOMY

A pupil controls the amount of light that enters the eye. A cat's pupil adjusts from large and round (for nighttime hunting) to a tiny slit (for walking around on a sunny day). That would be like having built-in night vision goggles or sunglasses! This, in turn, helps cats to be excellent nocturnal (nighttime) hunters.

Cat whiskers are powerful, too. Cats use them the same way we use our fingers to feel about in a dark room. Whiskers help wild cats hunt and move around at night. Of course, all cats have those sharp teeth, with powerful lower jaws that help cats to bite into and tear meat.

A tiger shows off his large ears, round eyes, whiskers, and sharp teeth.

A mother cheetah and her three cubs rest in the grasslands.

Another physical trait that all cat species share is fur. Fur protects a cat from temperature and weather changes. Think of a wild cat's fur as your rain jacket or winter coat. Fur also provides camouflage, helping cats blend in with their surroundings and hide from the animals they hunt (or animals that might hunt them). All cats have beautiful colors and patterns on their fur—from the varied coats of domestic striped tabby and black-and-white tuxedo cats to the gorgeous stripes of tigers and spots of cheetahs, cats are stunning creatures.

A baby bobcat, called a kitten,
climbs out of a hollow log.

CAT BEHAVIOR

HAVE YOU EVER WATCHED CATS at the zoo or on TV and compared them to your pet cat? Domesticated cats and wild cats behave in similar ways. Cats are natural predators, which means they will chase and pounce on things they see as potential food, or just when they're practicing their hunting skills.

You may have also noticed that cats sleep a lot. Wild cats need a lot of sleep to give them energy to hunt. But a cat's sleep is usually lighter and shorter than your night's sleep. This is because cats need to be able to wake at any moment to hunt their next meal or run from danger. Short naps are sometimes called "cat naps."

Another important cat behavior is the ability to climb thanks to a feature that all cats share: claws. Many cats live in or around forests because they use this climbing ability to their advantage.

Of course, some cats are better climbers than others. The heavier the cat is—like lions and tigers—the harder it is for them to move up and down a tree quickly. Cheetahs can't climb trees at all because their claws are non-retractable (that means they can't be pulled back under the skin). Instead of climbing, the cheetah uses its claws to grip the ground when it runs at top speed.

Claws are also important for scratching in self-defense and for catching prey.

CATS AS HUNTERS

CATS ARE EXCELLENT PREDATORS. Often, large cat species hunt animals that are larger than themselves.

So what makes them so skilled? First of all, they are able to move without being seen or heard. Not only are they quiet and able to sneak up on their prey, but the spots and striped patterns of their fur help them to blend in with their surroundings. You might wonder how such bold patterns can blend in, but they do. They actually mimic light patterns found in nature, helping to break up the outline of their bodies so prey can't spot them as easily.

The cheetah's spotted fur helps it blend in with its surroundings when hunting.

A male lion uses the tall grass to camouflage himself.

A lioness chases down a
cape buffalo for dinner.

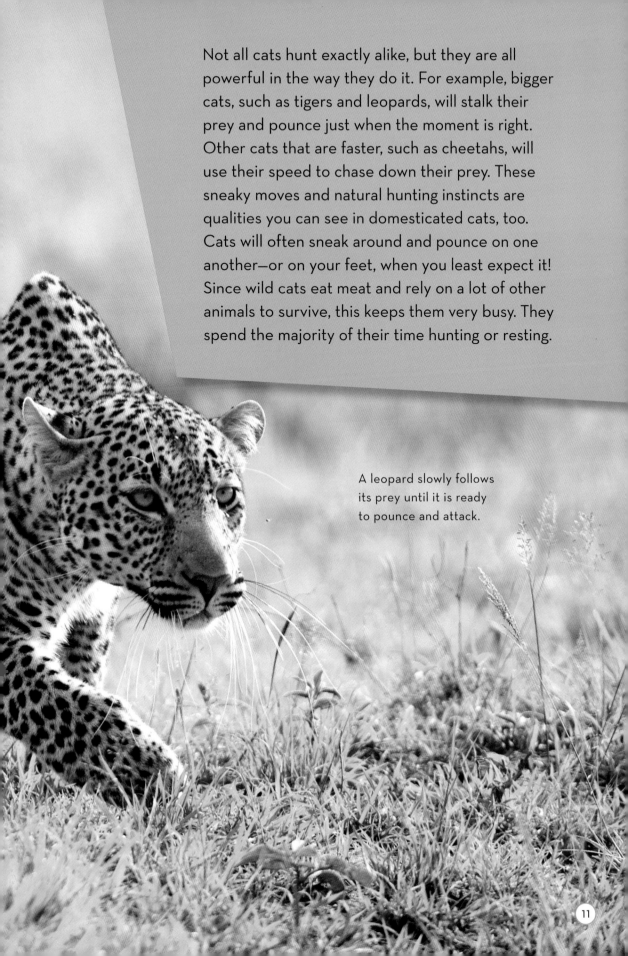

Not all cats hunt exactly alike, but they are all powerful in the way they do it. For example, bigger cats, such as tigers and leopards, will stalk their prey and pounce just when the moment is right. Other cats that are faster, such as cheetahs, will use their speed to chase down their prey. These sneaky moves and natural hunting instincts are qualities you can see in domesticated cats, too. Cats will often sneak around and pounce on one another—or on your feet, when you least expect it! Since wild cats eat meat and rely on a lot of other animals to survive, this keeps them very busy. They spend the majority of their time hunting or resting.

A leopard slowly follows its prey until it is ready to pounce and attack.

CAT COMMUNICATION

DOMESTICATED CATS MEOW, BUT SOME WILD CATS ARE FAMOUS FOR ANOTHER SOUND. The big and fierce roar! A roar is a well-known way that cats communicate, but only four species can roar: lions, tigers, jaguars, and leopards (although not the snow leopard).

So what makes it possible for these four cats to roar while others can't? It has to do with a specific area of their voice box, which helps to produce the sound. These four roaring species of cats are able to stretch their throats to make that deep roaring sound, something other wild cats are unable to do. Why do they roar? They usually do this to mark their territory and scare others away.

This Siberian tiger roars to warn other animals to stay away.

This caracal hisses at a photographer who got too close.

While other cats can't roar, many can still perform another very cat-like characteristic. They purr! Just like a roar, this purring is created in the voice box.

Of course, roaring and purring aren't the only sounds that cats make. Different cat species make a range of sounds, including hissing, snarling, grunting, moaning, and coughing to communicate a range of responses, from fear and self-defense to annoyance, and other moods.

A family of African lions communicates by snarling, moaning, and roaring at each other.

Tigers are true Big Cats.

What's the Difference?

IN ADDITION TO BEING REALLY COOL, the cat family can also be really confusing. Here's why. Have you ever heard of the term "big cats?" A lot of people use it to talk about any member of the cat family that is bigger than a domesticated cat. This means lions and tigers will often get lumped together with other large cat species.

Technically this isn't correct, though. To be a real "big cat," the species needs to be able to roar. If you go by this definition, only four cat species can do this: lions, tigers, jaguars, and leopards. This means species like cougars, snow leopards, and cheetahs aren't true "big cats." Sure, they are large, but since they can't roar, you can't call them a "big cat."

Strange, right? It's really not as complicated as it seems, and there is a trick to making it easier. Just use the term wild cats instead! Since all felines outside of domesticated cats can be defined as wild cats, it's an easy fix!

Though not technically a "big cat," snow leopards
are the most rarely seen of the wild cats.

THE FOUR BIG CATS

Lions

African lions are one of the most famous animals in Africa. One thing that sets them apart from other cats is that they gather together and travel in groups, called *prides*.

They are the only wild cat that does this. A pride is usually made up of four to six lions, along with their cubs. Together, they travel from one area to another, hunting animals such as zebras, wildebeests, buffaloes, and other mammals.

Male lions have large manes and generally weigh more than 400 pounds, while females lack manes and are smaller overall, closer to 280 pounds. The most well known kind of lion is the African lion, and you can also find the subspecies, the Asiatic lion, in India. (A subspecies is a population of a species that lives in a different place and has some different features than the main species.)

DID YOU KNOW?

Lions are great leapers. While they can't run as fast as cheetahs, lions can leap forward as far as 36 feet to tackle another animal to the ground. That's almost the length of a school bus!

Notice the differences between the male and female lion.

Tigers

Meet the largest member of the wild cat family—the tiger, which can weigh more than 600 pounds. In the tiger family, there are nine subspecies, all of which are endangered. Three other subspecies have gone extinct. Unlike lions, tigers usually travel alone, sticking to the cover of forests. Tigers can live in a variety of habitats: from reed beds in Central Asia to tropical rainforests in Southeast Asia to snowy forests in eastern Russia. They mostly hunt at night, eating anything from wild pigs to deer, and even smaller animals like birds, fish, and monkeys.

The most common and recognized subspecies of tiger is the Bengal tiger. The other eight subspecies still alive today include the Sumatran and Siberian tigers. And if you're wondering what a white tiger is, it's just a color variation of the Bengal tiger, bred by people in captivity.

All tiger species have orange fur with white undersides and black stripes.

A tiger stalks through the grass

Leopards

A leopard paces the base of a tree.

This is one big cat that definitely relies on its climbing abilities. Leopards will even take the prey they kill into the treetops with them to eat. These cats range from about 60 to 200 pounds, and their diet consists of anything from beetles and small mammals to creatures much bigger than themselves, like antelope. Leopards are found in areas of Africa, West Asia, the Middle East, and South Asia. A leopard's habitat can vary from tropical rainforests to deserts and even cold mountains. Some leopards can even have mostly dark fur. Often found in deep forests, these leopards are called black panthers. Many leopard populations have been hunted a great deal and are considered near threatened.

Up in a tree, a young leopard feeds on an impala.

This wild cat, commonly called a black jaguar, has spots hidden in its mostly dark fur.

Jaguars

The jaguar is the only true big cat of the Americas, and you can find it in much of South America and parts of North America. A few have even been spotted in the Southwestern United States in parts of Arizona, California, New Mexico and Texas! If you take a quick glance at the jaguar, you might think you're looking at a leopard. Both have circles made up of black spots called rosettes, but the jaguar usually has smaller black spots inside the rosette.

This can be hard to see, so there are other traits you can look for. The jaguar is stockier and heavier than the leopard, weighing around 120 pounds, to more than 300. Jaguars also have shorter tails than most leopards. Like black leopards, jaguars can also be melanistic (black in color).

The jaguar prefers watery environments, such as swamps, for its habitat. Like other big cats, it will hunt both small and larger mammals, including peccaries and deer. Jaguars also feed on reptiles and regularly prey on caimans (kay-mans), cousins of alligators.

A jaguar's spots will have a smaller black spot inside the rosette.

A jaguar hunts near a stream in Brazil.

NORTH AMERICA'S WILD CATS

YOU ALREADY KNOW ABOUT THE ONE TRUE BIG CAT that can be found in parts of North America, the jaguar, but there are a few other cat species that also call the continent home. The first is the *mountain lion*, which also goes by several other names, including puma, cougar, and panther. It can weigh more than 200 pounds, and is known for living in both mountains and forests in the Western United States.

Another wild cat is the *lynx*, which is mostly found in cold areas such as Canada and Alaska. Lynxes are listed as threatened in the lower 48 states but they can sometimes be spotted there. This species relies on small mammals such as hares, rabbits, and birds to survive.

The other wild cat in North America is the *bobcat*, which is one of the smallest, at just 2 to 3 feet long and 20 to 30 pounds. Bobcats are found in most of the United States and Mexico, and they hunt prey such as birds, mice, rabbits, and sometimes animals as large as deer.

A few smaller cats will show up in the United States from time to time. They aren't as well known as the ones listed above, but you can put the *jaguarundi*, *ocelot*, and *margay* on this list.

The lynx's gray and brown fur helps it blend in with its snowy environment.

A mountain lion walks across the snow.

A bobcat scents the air for signs of prey.

OTHER WILD CATS

YOU CAN FIND ANOTHER FEW DOZEN WILD CATS THROUGHOUT THE WORLD, and they're definitely worth learning about. The *caracal* (also called the desert lynx) is one of the most interesting-looking wild cats, with its long, tufted ears. It's found in Africa and parts of Asia.

The one that probably looks most like a domesticated cat is actually called a *wildcat*. It's the ancestor of the pet cats we know today. It has a gray-brown coat with dark striping on the legs and is even the size of most pet cats, around 7 to 20 pounds, and only a couple of feet long.

The *ocelot* (oss-lot), also similar in size to a large domesticated cat, is one of the most wildly patterned cats. It has both spots and stripes, and is mostly found in South America and it will sometimes go as far north as Texas.

The *margay* looks similar to an ocelot and shares much of the same habitat territory, but it is smaller.

The margay is a small wild cat species found in South and Central America and Mexico.

A caracal perches on a tree.

This cat might look like a pet,
but it's actually a wildcat.

HISTORY OF CATS

THE WILD CATS WE KNOW AND LOVE TODAY are just a sampling of all the different species that used to live on our planet. Cats have been around for millions of years, and there used to be a lot more of them, both in overall numbers and different types.

Let's take a look at some of those wild cats that are now extinct (no longer alive). During the time of the Ice Age 2.6 million years ago, there was a huge cat that would roam North America, called the *American lion*. Don't let the name throw you off; there's actually a lot of debate as to whether this creature was more like a lion or a jaguar. Either way, scientists believe this cat weighed more than 1,000 pounds.

Another well-known type of feline were the saber-toothed cats. There were many subspecies including saber-toothed tigers, but all are extinct today. You've probably seen pictures of saber-toothed tigers with their extra-long fangs coming out the front of their mouths. Both saber-toothed cats and the American lion went extinct 10,000 to 11,000 years ago.

Some of the other wild cats that have gone extinct include the Pleistocene tiger, cave lion, and *Machairodus kabir*, which many scientists believe was actually an early saber-toothed cat species. There was also the giant jaguar and giant cheetah, both almost twice as big as the modern-day versions of these animals.

The skull of a saber-toothed cat tells scientists a lot about this extinct cat species, including the kind of food it probably ate.

CONSERVATION FOR CATS

Road signs, like this cougar crossing sign in Florida, help educate people about the presence of wild cats.

WILD CATS ARE FACING THREATS and the populations of many species are declining. Habitat loss and illegal hunting are two of the biggest causes. Today, most wild cat species are considered at risk. Some are considered endangered or threatened, including lions, tigers, snow leopards, cheetahs, and lynx. **Endangered** means a species is close to becoming extinct. **Threatened** means a species is declining so fast that it could soon become endangered. Many wild cat species are **vulnerable** to extinction if the problems they face don't improve.

To help protect wild cats, there are many groups dedicated to educating people about the problems of wild cats and how they can help. For instance, the National Wildlife Federation helps mountain lions by restoring their habitat and providing ways for people to safely coexist with them. The National Wildlife Federation is the driving force behind the effort to create what will be one of the only wildlife highway overpasses in the United States, which will allow mountain lions and other wildlife to safely cross a busy freeway in California.

Cheetahs are one of the
species of wild cats that
are currently threatened by
habitat loss and illegal hunting.

HOW YOU CAN HELP

It's a little scary to think that some of these big, beautiful animals might not be around in the future if we don't do something to protect them. We need to work together to protect these animals and their habitats. And you can help, too!

A leopard stares down the camera and gives a warning roar.

1. You've already taken the first step by educating yourself about wild cats. Not everyone knows that many wild cat species are in trouble. Now you can teach your friends and family members about why wild cats are so cool and why they need our help. The more people understand about these amazing animals, the easier it is to make choices that protect wild cat species.

Tourists observe this tiger from a safe distance in a wildlife sanctuary.

2. Make better entertainment decisions with your family. Visit wild cats in zoos with large natural enclosures or out in the wild in National Parks, rather than places that make cats perform tricks or allow people to take pictures with these potentially dangerous wild animals.

3. Ask your parents to help you write a letter to your local senator, congressman, or even your favorite celebrity, to inform them about what is going on with wild cat populations. Ask this person to use his or her voice and influence to help bring an end to illegal hunting and protect the rainforests, mountains, and grasslands that wild cats call home. You could also ask your teacher to help you get your classmates involved in a letter writing campaign to save the wild cats!

A baby snow leopard watches cautiously from the trees.

MORE WAYS YOU CAN HELP

A tiger takes a swim.

4. There are hundreds of organizations all over the world working every day to save wild cats and big cats, including the National Wildlife Federation, the National Geographic Society Big Cats Initiative, FOUR PAWS, and Panthera. Choose an organization (local, national, non-profit) close to your hometown and contact it to learn more about how you can help protect the world's wild cat populations and save their habitats no matter where you live. You could volunteer your time or hold a fundraiser to help pay for their important work.

5. Be a wild cat warrior: Defend wild cats by speaking out. If you see anyone abusing or doing something that could endanger these incredible and valuable creatures, always report it to the proper authorities.

This mountain lion watches the photographer.

- Most people don't realize that many wild cats are good swimmers.

Tigers are good swimmers.

- Except for the lion, wild cats prefer to be alone—hunting, sleeping, and living on their own.

- Another thing that sets lions apart from other cats is the tufts of fur at the tip of their tails.

Lions prefer to live in groups called prides.

Think twice before challenging a cheetah to a race!

- A cheetah can reach speeds of over 60 miles per hour, making it the fastest mammal on land!

- All cats (including our pets) have a very well-developed sense of smell, made even stronger by a special smell-taste organ in the roof of their mouth called the Jacobson's organ.

- When a lion roars, it can be heard from as far away as 5 miles.

- The jaguar has a very strong jaw, making its bite stronger than a hippo's!

Jaguar shows off his strong jaw with a big yawn!

- Tiger populations have taken a big hit in recent years, mostly due to disease and habitat loss. Between 1900 and 2000, the numbers went from roughly 100,000 to around 3,500.

This tiger mom sits patiently while her cubs practice teething.

- Tiger stripes are very unique; no two sets are alike, so they're kind of like fingerprints in a way.

- Jaguars are known for pouncing, which relates to their name. Jaguar is a Native American word that translates to "he who kills with one leap."